"Denial's Veil: Unmasking Government Distortions"

TABLE OF CONTENTS

There has never been a time before that I have thoroughly enjoyed both researching and imparting to an audience my own thoughts and feelings as much as I did in this book that you hold in your hands. If you derive even half the pleasure from reading it as I did from creating it, I will be ecstatic. The book that you hold in your hands has been a long overdue hallmark attributable to our society. Please bear in mind however your presuppositions happen to be, your perspective will be better for reading this book.

PROLOGUE

Have you ever sat and pondered about the future of our world or how about your own near future? Since I was a young man, I have done just that. I have now come to the realization that I can no longer sit idly by and watch my world be led to the slaughter by its government…

INTRODUCTION

Each one of us is in a state of what I call denial. Let's expound upon this very real and conscious state of mind if I may. Is the state of mind we are all in simply the refusal to acknowledge the existence or severity of unpleasant external realities of internal thoughts and feelings? Or could there be a simpler explanation here such that we are all in a state of self-perpetuating fear of the truth that if realized would force upon us a reality too close to home to accept? Well, I plan to unravel a few realities which have served well as facets of the denial gripping most of us (simple and hardworking Americans). The first and one of the most pressing realities which I am going to shed light on are those which our government distort for their own means and in turn exploit the average citizen as a result. Let us consider a topic that is at least a weekly struggle for most of us. This topic is whether to put gas in our automobiles or to pay our bills each month. A new survey reflects that more than three-fourths of Americans don't have enough money saved to pay their bills for six months to include households with joint income, according to survey results released by Bankrate, Inc. which is one of the Web's leading aggregator of financial rate information, offering an unparalleled depth and breadth of rate data and financial content. It is not a secret that an exceptionally large majority of our population lives paycheck to paycheck as well, which only complicates paying our bills on time. It is from my own personal experience that when I was in the boat of living paycheck to paycheck that I purposely put off paying my essential bills on time because I simply could not afford to do so. Every time I delayed paying my bills on time such as basic utilities like gas and electricity; I had to, out of necessity cut my spending elsewhere to eventually pay those bills I had put off. The stark reality is that many of us are in this very real and pressing circumstance every month and yet we all come back to the basic question of putting food on our table for our families meaning not paying our rent/mortgage thus risking eviction or paying our essential bill(s) on time and going without food. Do we all believe that Big Oil and our government are separate entities? The government would have you believe that the union or marriage if you will that it has with "Big Oil" is inextricable. Well, I do believe this is the case, if not simply a false truth that we citizens have been duped into accepting as truth. Is it too much to ask that we as citizens should have the right to choose how much we fork out for the fuel we put into our vehicles?! Ok so; what is the big deal with "Big Oil" and why are gas prices so damn high? I will tell you, because our government is in bed with Big Oil and our elected officials will continue this relationship. We can't count on politicians of either party to do anything serious against the energy companies. "Big Oil" as I call it is an entity made up of huge corporations who in turn lobby in congress with what seems an unlimited revenue stream against the citizens in this country thus keeping a very oppressive price of gas at the pump. This lobbying is when these huge corporations pay our government exorbitant amounts of money which goes directly into the politicians' pockets as aforementioned. The purpose of lobbying is to persuade by whatever means possible a legislating body to buy off on an agenda being lobbied for by the lobbyist which in this case happens to be "Big Oil". The government in this case is paid to push such an agenda and to have complete disregard for doing what is right for the citizens; the government pockets the money and economic exploitation ensues forcing the citizens of such a government to pay a variable price at the pump. This relationship which our own government and "Big Oil" has and will continue unless we direct our attention at our elected officials and demand separation of Big Oil and government and demand honest representation! It would be remiss of me if I did not harp on the very real fact that we are all slaves to that which should be subject to our scrutiny. In other words, that which should be voted upon by the people is simply swept under the rug and distorted by our government for their own means.

HISTORICAL CONTEXT

Are we all descendent from monkeys? The government would like us to believe that beyond any doubt the monkey you saw in the zoo the other day is a distant cousin of yours and mine. I am incredibly astounded by the extreme measures our government will take just to keep free thought out of public education and discouraged among its citizens for that matter. Dr. Colen Patterson, a senior paleontologist for the British Museum of Natural History, in a public lecture before the American Museum of Natural History in New York

City said that he asked the geology staff of the Field Museum of Natural History this question: Can you tell me anything you know about evolution, any one thing that is true? He asked the same question of evolutionists that met at the Evolutionary Morphology Seminar at the University of Chicago. The answer he received from both groups was silence, except that one member of the Morphology Seminar said: I know one thing- it ought not to be taught in high school. How correctly Arlen Carlblom wrote in the Mankato,

Minnesota, Free Press. I have taught my children to believe that the Bible is the exact Word of God. When public schools promote evolution, it undermines my children's faith in me. If the atheist child has the right not to be indoctrinated with Christian ideas, my child has the right not to be indoctrinated with the anti-Bible views supported by the theory of evolution. Supreme Court Justice Abe Fortas summed it up correctly when he said in connection with the Supreme Court ruling (1981) about the Arkansas antievolution law:

Government is our democracy…state and federal…must be neutral in matters of religious theory… It may not aid, foster, or promote one religious theory as against another. This includes the evolutionary theory, idea, or belief over against any other belief. Teaching evolution over against the teaching of the Bible is worse than, and as unconstitutional as Lutherans teaching their belief in public schools over against Roman Catholicism, or Jews teaching their beliefs over against Christianity, and vice versa.

Simply elementary justice demands that tax money be paid by Christian citizens should not be used by schools to destroy the Christian faith of the children of these taxpayers. – Albert Sippert, From Eternity to Eternity (1989) When I attended public school as a young boy, I found myself in more than a few tiffs with my teachers simply because I disagreed with what they taught, or force fed me in class. The entire claim of evolutionists is based on assumptions, including millions and billions of years. Dr. E. H. Andrews, professor at the

University of London, said that even the timescale and radiometric dating used by the evolutionists is questioned. He said that such dating which gives hundreds of millions of years to fossil bearing rocks is based on assumptions and that these assumptions cannot be justified scientifically. Because evolution has no scientific evidence for its beliefs and because it cannot give scientific answers to origins and is based merely on assumptions, it is not scientific. When evolutionists assume something to be fact without positive proof, they are resorting to nonscientific methods to set up something as a scientific fact. Evolution is an assumption, a speculation, a belief. Stretching the imagination, it might be called a philosophy, but it is not science. It has rightly been referred to as a new kind of mythology. – Albert Sippert, From Eternity to Eternity (1989) to endorse the idea of evolution is to essentially disown any possibility that you ever had a purpose on this earth to begin with. You are no longer that unique snowflake that your mother called you when you were younger. The belief of evolution is equal to being an atheist; both beliefs are baseless and have no origin. As early as first grade and reaching through most our country's universities are implanting teachers and professors both who have agreed as a prerequisite of being hired that they will teach the rhetoric of evolution in the classroom. The scary aspect about evolution is that it is preached as the only process of origin of our species and is defended beyond reason by prejudiced teachers. This belief is flourishing only because we have allowed it to do so. How do you ask? Well, our tax dollars do go towards the public school system, however, not in the productive way you and I would have intended. A good percentage of our tax dollars go towards inflating the theory of evolution in every subject, not just biology or history but math and science as well. The government would never endorse such a lie in the first place if such would mean admitting that we are no better than animals, well monkeys in this case. I will go as far as to say evolution being taught to a child is no better than teaching your own child that the color of their skin is good and pure and everyone who is different is bad and evil. A child sees things for how they are on the surface and does not form prejudices beforehand. We as a collective nation of independent thinkers should demand that our government stop the spreading of deception in our schools. The scary thought that my future children will be exposed to blatant propaganda in their school is too terrible to imagine.

TYPES OF CORRUPTION

God is secondary to our goals and aspirations in this world or rather the government would like you to believe that God has nothing to do with your path in life. The separation of church and state is how it should be. James Madison, the primary author of the Constitution of the United States, said this: "We have staked the whole future of our new nation NOT upon the power of government; far from it. We have staked the future of all our political constitutions upon the capacity of each of ourselves to govern ourselves according to the moral principles of the Ten Commandments." There is coming a day when you will be persecuted and prosecuted for simply endorsing the idea that God created the world, and that the government is wrong. Why not embrace a universal belief that takes precedence over your own faith?! The government has sole discretion of all spending about our tax dollars for whatever floats the "Governments boat". Have no fear, our government will ensure that our rights are protected. If only this was the truth, however, you and I both know it is not. You have God inside of you and therefore you are God. All of these are blatant lies that each one of us goes along with. First, let's address the very real and present danger which is that our government would be more than accommodating to ban God from all institutions both public and private. Let's take this one step further, our government would be all to obliging if every citizen renounced any belief in God period and this would make you a more subservient citizen with which the government could do what they wish. Is it possible for both church and state to co-exist; the government will fight tooth and nail to convince you that it would truly be an unholy alliance if anything. You know as well as I that when the government starts to mandate you pay a tax based on whether you disavow your Christian beliefs that the time of individual freedoms is pretty much over. Wake up people! The land of the free as we once called it is soon to be wishful thinking from our past. Our forebears authored the Declaration of Independence with clear direction from God himself. George Washington, appealed to God while he was President "Almighty God; We make our earnest prayer that Thou wilt keep the United States in Thy holy protection; that Thou wilt incline the hearts of the citizens to cultivate a spirit of subordination and obedience to government; and entertain a brotherly affection and love for one another and for their fellow citizens of the United States at large. And finally, that Thou wilt most graciously be pleased to dispose us all to do justice, to love mercy, and to demean ourselves with that charity, humility, and pacific temper of mind which were the characteristics of the Divine Author of our blessed religion, and without a humble imitation of whose example in these things we can never hope to be a happy nation. Grant our supplication, we beseech Thee, through Jesus Christ our Lord. Amen." Every other day I watch as Congress continually denigrates the very essence of the Constitution which was intended to stress God. I do believe that our government has reached a stage of no return in-regards to allowing God to be the forefront of anything much less our own government.

THE IMPACT ON SOCIETY

When was the last time the IRS was audited? Is our government allowed by law to go on billion-dollar spending sprees with our tax dollars? I am sure you will agree with me that the answer is no. Last time I checked the only liberty the government could take with our tax dollars was to support the common defense and infrastructure which includes schools, roads, parks, etc. A large amount of all our tax dollars goes directly into the pockets of our elected politicians who in turn author bills which specifically include earmarks from our tax dollars to justify what they have pocketed. Earmarks are projects that receive federal funding, primarily at the request of one or more members of Congress, typically for work done inside a requesting Member's district or State. Earmarks may direct spending to a particular entity or take the form of a targeted tax or tariff measure that benefits one or a few entities. Because earmarks can benefit one or a narrow range of beneficiaries, they are seldom the subject of Congressional hearing or debates as bills move through the Congressional process, and therefore the legislative record for most earmarks is sparse. While most earmark requests are sent by requesting Members to the relevant committees of jurisdiction early in the legislative process, House and Senate rules only require certain information on earmark requests to be made available to the public, and it can be difficult even for Members of Congress to examine each project before votes are cast on bills that authorize or appropriate earmarks. – Information provided by Taxpayers for

Common Sense. "TCS FY2010 Earmark Analysis: Apples-to-Apples Increase in Earmarks, "February 17, 2010. What does all that mumbo jumbo tell you? Well, it tells me quite clearly that our government can legislate or pass bills that include earmarks with or without the public knowing about it. It also tells me that when I decipher the convoluted policies of our government that I discover that these earmarks are a way of exploiting the average hard working tax paying citizen by taking the form of targeted taxes. This is absurd; on the one hand our government is allowed to legislate into law bills which put extra money in their pockets and take from us in the form of additional/special taxes... On the other hand, are these the same congressperson or legislatures if you will be there to create laws and bills for our benefit?! Could you survive if you suddenly lost your source of income whether it be income from the government, for example unemployment or from your job? Most people would be up the creek without a paddle or a boat for that matter. Our country is a bubble just waiting to pop. Our government is in debt up to its eyeballs and when our debt bubble explodes so does our society. Life is fine and dandy one moment and then all of the sudden you find your city in complete anarchy because the price of a loaf of bread is now $100 dollars and gas is only for those with more cash than you have ever seen or a resource worth trading for it. Let's look at another startling fact that we hard working citizens have chosen to ignore or even worse be in ignorance about. Our governments' current plan is to ensure every citizen of this nation eventually falls into complete servitude or slavery if you will. How you ask will this mission be conducted; well just look at the debt that not only most Americans have and couple that specifically with student debt and bank debt, but our countries balance sheet is also insurmountable by any means. What rights do you as citizens really think you have… the right to sleep in your own bed, the right to eat what you want or more simply the right to exist? I am appalled by what few rights we do have and how our government will fight tooth and nail to rescind as many rights as they can and as fast as they can without even blinking an eye. We must all awake and take to the streets in protest in every city of our Nation. Our very livelihood is at stake and doing nothing will only further ensure the inevitable servitude we have and will endure into the future as enemies of the state. A government for the people and by the people is legal and forthright. We have a government which is for the elected officials and against the people. The day that our government begins to label you and me as terrorists simply because our opinions or viewpoints differ with theirs is the day, we give up all rights as a citizen. There will come a time soon that our government will make such demands of its citizens that if not agreed upon will result in indefinite imprisonment or even death. We are living in a time when our government has become so large and so oppressive to the point that the will of the citizens is simply squashed and not given an audience. There will come a time when all citizens of this government will be faced with the choice of supporting their family which will mean compromising your values and swearing complete allegiance to the system which enslaves you or starving because of your noncompliance. The time of fear mongering and massive exploitation of a country's citizen rights has come. The troops will be out in force patrolling your neighborhood sooner than you think. Whose job is it to protect yourself and your family… the government? No! Whose job is it to ensure your family does not go hungry?

If you guessed the government, then you would be wrong. There are too many in this country that have long been dependent upon our government for well fair and social security which only inflates our governments own hubris and will bite these unsuspecting citizens in the butt leading to enslavement or even death. We were wrong to set up a government to begin with and not pursue our own goals separate from governance.

There is something very wrong with this country; I am not talking about the crime epidemic or obesity epidemic for that matter. I am talking about things that are being disintegrated in front of our very eyes such as the American dream of home ownership or the liberty to pray in public. Are we ready for our very human rights that exist separate from the government to be repudiated? I don't think we are. We must hold our local government's first ransom for the unconscionable which has happened in the past and will happen again. We can then rise as citizens with a will that cannot be broken or trampled on by the government ever again.

Would you willfully allow someone to come into your house and rape your wife and then rob you of your goods? I didn't think so. This is exactly what the government is doing to these countries' hard-working families, and we need to start seeing things for how they really are. On average, every great nation has stood for approximately 200 hundred years until they declined and ultimately collapsed entirely. These nations have progressed in this sequence: From bondage to spiritual faith; from faith to great courage; from courage to liberty; from liberty to abundance; from abundance to selfishness; from selfishness to Complacency; from complacency to apathy; from apathy to dependency; from dependency back to bondage. – Alexander Fraser Tyler, Cycle of Democracy (1770). Well, our time is right around the corner if we do not fight back in these perilous times. A wise man once said the following: The future is unfolding before one's eyes and cannot be foretold or determined." I came up with that quote years prior as a child. Think about it though, we as citizens of this country ensure at least a fair future for ourselves, if any that is if we fight against tyranny and if not for ourselves then for our heirs. Let's look at another startling fact that we hard working citizens have chosen to ignore or even worse be in ignorance about. Our governments' current plan is to ensure every citizen of this nation eventually falls into complete servitude or slavery if you will.

How you ask will this mission be conducted; well just look at the debt that not only most Americans have and couple that specifically with student debt and bank debt, but our countries balance sheet is also insurmountable by any means. When the majority of such a population is satiated by debt that has essentially become a "way of life", this problem is what crushes all rights and civil liberties thus enabling the government to seize total control.

ROOT CAUSES

Have you ever wondered about what you would do if you won the lottery, I mean the big jackpot?! Would you save half of the winnings and invest the other half, or would you impart the things that you have won to a charity? These are all questions that I have pondered. There does not seem to be a precipice that one can reach which ensures inner peace. I mean, we will never be happy with just getting that next promotion or larger house or new car…etc. The list can go on indefinitely although the point at hand is that we will never be satisfied with just what we have so to speak. Our insatiable needs are and will always be unquenchable. The government which we have allowed to be in power will continue to quest for power and domination and in doing so try to take everything from you and me. The overreaching powers of such a government will keep the impoverished and indebted citizens of this country subservient from this generation to the next if we insist on living largely above our means. Many young people today going to college, for example, have with

great intention borrowed
hundreds of thousands of dollars
in loans to be able to afford
college to begin with. This on
the one hand has potentially
offered the young woman or
man the educational opportunity
and leverage of making a great
life for themselves post college
education, however, due to the
insurmountable student debt
plus interest that amounts upon
these earnest young students
their financial future is now
destroyed for life. Attaining
even this basic college degree
such as a bachelor's means
getting into debt for most

students. Students who graduate in 2013 owe $26,000 on average in student loans, according to a recent Fidelity survey. Student debt surpasses government-issued loans, private loans, and credit card debt. Student debt is now adding a new dimension to an ever-growing problem. These students are now debt slaves to a system which on the surface promises a bright future but a harsh devastated future of destitution and servitude. Are you one of these individuals still holding on to that shred of hope yet struggling to keep your head above water in all respects? It is, regrettably, no exaggeration to say that we are living in a time of irrationality, deception, confusion, anger, and unfocused fear — an ominous combination, with few precedents. There has never been a time when it was so important to have a voice of sanity, insight, and understanding of what is happening in the world. Our world certainly abounds with opportunity and a great step in the right direction is attaining a college degree. However, a college degree is not worth its weight in credit hours if you end up in debt up to your eyeballs in the process. Going back to the subject of this chapter which is incontinence; our society will never draw the line on when is enough with anything for that matter. This makes for individuals borrowing loan after loan and swiping credit cards indiscriminately which invariably has led to and leads to a society as a whole bankrupt and indebt for all foreseeable futures. I simply wish to make clear what has become an extremely fast and furious locomotive of our society is debt and our debt locomotive is heading towards the cliff of death without regard. Oh... you say that debt is not an issue for you; well, let's look at that for a second. Do you own a house or even rent for that matter?

How about ownership of an automobile? If your answer to one of these questions is yes, then you are potentially part of the majority of which I have been referring to thus far. Have you paid off in full for your property? If yes, then you are not whom I am referring to. If not, you are indeed in debt whether it is to the loan holder of your mortgage or the loan holder of your automobile or even to the rental company of your apartment for the contract you signed prior to moving in. You see very clearly that most of the population is in debt of some sort and will continue to be in debt short of winning the lottery or divine intervention.

CASE STUDIES

Have you noticed that the market is so incredibly inundated with low interest loans left, and right?! Well, this is indeed the case. You can reach a 30-year mortgage at a loan interest rate now that would not have been possible for the last decade. Do not be fooled; that low interest mortgage you have will not pay off in the end. In fact, by the time you are done paying your home mortgage down, you will have paid probably close to four times the original amount you paid for the property plus interest. The generation we live

in is by far the most exploited
generation to date. I wish I
could go back in time and undo
my decision to buy a home; I
mean, homeownership is great
but is the value worth going into
debt for? Let me tell you a little
bit about my financial savvy. I
grew up in a modest household
where both my parents worked,
and the result was a nice warm
meal three times per day which
was great for me. My work ethic
I owe to my parents because I
was always told since I was
young that nothing worth
having ever comes easy; this I
have learned over my few adult

years is quite true indeed. Anyway, I digress; my discipline with money came later in life when I had my first career. I learned the value of money and that saving that money I earned not only compounded interest but has given me peace of mind for volatile economic times. Can the value of the dollar bill really be subject to what the masses in the populace think of it?! Well… yes, our fiat currency was backed by gold or the gold standard if you will until 1971 when former President Nixon officially ended the gold standard. The ubiquitous result was a significant devaluation of our dollar or in other words the amount of stuff we used to be able to buy with our dollar has now significantly decreased. The Federal Reserve System fulfills its public mission as an independent entity within government. It is not "owned" by anyone and is not a private, profit-making institution. As the nation's central bank, the Federal Reserve derives its authority from the Congress of the United States. It is considered an independent central bank because its monetary policy decisions do not have to be approved by the President or anyone else in the executive or legislative branches of government, it does not receive funding appropriated by the Congress, and the terms of the members of the Board of Governors span multiple presidential and congressional terms. How does that sit with you? Well, I will tell you that due to the lack of regulation of the Federal Reserve it simply means that this entity can print as much money as they want for as long as they want aka pumping which in-turn makes our dollar bill worthless. "The U.S. government has a technology, called a printing press (or today, its electronic equivalent), that allows it to produce as many U.S. dollars as it wishes at no cost."- Ben Bernanke, Federal Reserve Chairman (2005-current) how can this be you might ask? Well, the belief that the dollar has any value more than what we the citizens intrinsically assign it is like the belief in Santa Clause for an ignorant child; if enough children believe St. Nick exists then he must exist right? No! The same applies with our currency, the value is based on enough of the general populace believing that it has value, but we are as disillusioned as the children believing in Santa Clauses existence.

THE PANDERER IN CHIEF

I would be lying to you if I said I would hate to have everything supported me on a silver platter by my own government. This is a stretch however because you and I both know our government has been giving handouts in every form possible for years now especially from 2009 on when our country gained a new commander- in- chief or as I like to refer to him as the panderer-in-chief. As of the latest data released by the United States Department of

Agriculture, the total is 47.6 million individuals of whom are on food stamps, which is more than the entire populations of many large nations. A program with this many participants incurs huge administrative costs: $3.8 billion in 2012 – and that is only the federal government's share. Just think about how much more in taxes we citizens will end up paying. States are allowed to deny food stamps to convicted felons. Different states have different policies; however, it doesn't affect their expenditures either way since the USDA (United

States Department of Agriculture) pays for all food stamps. This current administration loosened the ABAWD (able-bodied adults without dependents) requirements. This action was like extending unemployment benefits due to the poor job market.

In other words, our government has made it that much easier to get on a subsistence program such as food stamps and in the meantime enslaves more unsuspecting citizens in a system they will never get out of. Our president betrays all of us hard working tax paying citizens and expects our full subservient allegiance to his every whim. Consider the following quotes from notable figures in our history: "Dictatorship naturally arises out of democracy, and the most aggravated form of tyranny and slavery out of the most extreme liberty." – Plato, Ancient Greek Philosopher (428 BC-348 BC). "Power is not a means, it is an end. One does not establish a dictatorship in order to safeguard a revolution; one makes the revolution in order to establish the dictatorship."-George Orwell, English Novelist (1903-1950). The problem that exists is farther reaching than you or I can even understand. It is more a fundamental problem our government bases their shrewd choices on. The fact is that our government looks at its citizens like cattle and simply herding us will not suffice any longer. I for one am not a follower simply because it is the expectation to do so. We are inherently free to think what we want and to do what we want as long that we do not infringe on others, right?

God gave every one of us free will and the last time I checked our free will cannot be revoked by our government.

EPILOGUE

"Since mankind's dawn, a handful of oppressors have accepted the responsibility over our lives that we should have accepted for ourselves. By doing so, they took our power. By doing nothing, we gave it away. We've seen where their way leads, through camps and wars, towards the slaughterhouse."

\- Alan Moore, *V for Vendetta*

ABOUT THE AUTHOR

With over a decade of successful management and leadership experience, the author has built a reputation for meeting the most challenging organizational goals and objectives. Known for a pragmatic and focused approach, Michael Ricci has been recognized for turning seemingly impossible situations into triumphs of ingenuity and determination.

As an author, his work reflects this depth of insight, tackling complex themes of government control and corruption with a deft hand.

In his latest book, "My Best Friend Denial," Michael invites readers to explore the intricate dance of power and its impact on the human spirit. This book is not just a testament to their expertise but also a beacon for those who seek truth amidst the tumult of societal discourse.

*PAGE LEFT BLANK
INTENTIONALLY*

PAGE LEFT BLANK
INTENTIONALLY